Animals
That Make Me Say
WOW!

NATIONAL
WILDLIFE
FEDERATION.

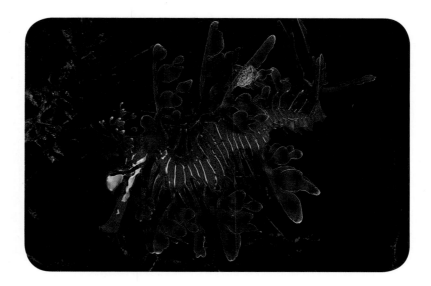

Dawn Cusick

imagine!
Publishing

Image copyrights held by the photographers on page 79

Text Copyright © 2014 by Dawn Cusick

An Imagine Book
Published by Charlesbridge
85 Main Street
Watertown, MA 02472
(617) 926-0329
www.charlesbridge.com

Library of Congress Cataloging-in-Publication Data
is available upon request.

ISBN: 978-1-62354-041-8

Printed in China. Manufactured in June, 2014.

(hc) 10 9 8 7 6 5 4 3 2 1

Display type and text type set in Motter Corpus and Frutiger.

Jacket and Type Design: Megan Kirby
Proofreading: Brett Blofield
Produced by EarlyLight Books

For information about custom editions, special sales,
premium and corporate purchases, please contact
Charlesbridge Publishing at specialsales@charlesbridge.com

Contents

Introduction

Welcome to a world that will make you say WOW!

We share Earth with millions of animals. In most places, there is not enough food and habitat to go around, and animals use some amazing adaptations in their bodies and behaviors to help them compete.

Alligators and crocodiles, for example, use bumps on their scales called dermal receptors to pick up movement by predators and prey. Herons and egrets stand on the backs of hippopotamuses to safely search for food, and some young crabs use jellyfish and anemones for protection.

On your mark . . . get set . . . say WOW!

Defense WOW!

DEFENSE: the ways organisms protect themselves from predators and their environment

From treetop hideaways to stinky sprays, animal defenses can make you say WOW! Animals use amazing behavior and anatomy adaptations to protect their homes, get food, fight predators, and more.

Safe Snooze

Some large mammals sleep away the hot parts of the day up high in trees, where few predators can reach them. When it's time to climb down, the animals need sharp claws, strong muscles, and good balance! Leopards can go down trees head first, while bears wrap their paws around the tree and scoot down, a little at a time.

 **Defense** WOW!

Muscle Cats

Leopards often carry recently killed prey up trees to prevent other animals from stealing their food. Impressed? Wait until you hear this: leopards can carry prey that weighs three times their weight more than 20 feet high. Multiply your weight by three; how much weight could you carry up a tree if you were a leopard?

Defense WOW!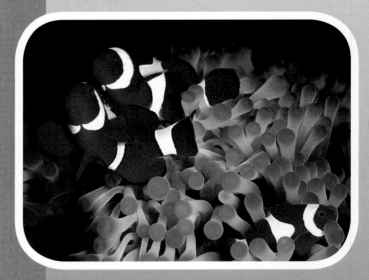

Good for You, Good For Me

A clownfish's relationship with the sea anemone is an example of mutualism. Anemones give the clownfish protection from predators. The sea anemones receive extra oxygen from the clownfish's moving fins. Clownfish also help anemones by eating parasites on them.

Cool Mucus!

Clownfish escape predators by living between the tentacles of sea anemones. Ordinary fish would be stung by the anemone, but clownfish secrete special mucus that prevents stings. Young clownfish begin making this mucus when they are stung for the first time.

With Friends Like These . . .

The tops and undersides of jellyfish make safe hiding places for young crabs. Jellyfish stinging cells (called nematocytes) are found in their tentacles, and cannot reach the crabs. As the crabs get older, their exoskeletons harden, protecting them from the stinging cells in jellyfish, coral, and sea anemones.

Tree House Nests

Newborn squirrels are very small, weighing about half an ounce. They do not have fur, and their eyes and ears are closed, so baby squirrels need protection from predators and bad weather. Moms build nests in tree holes or in leaves, where the babies will live for their first seven weeks.

Defense **WOW!**

great
horned
owls

Recycling Nests

Many mammals and birds make dens and nests in trees. Sometimes they do their own building, but often they recycle dens and nests abandoned by other animals.

Foxes dig dens to raise their kits, or use dens abandoned by badgers or woodchucks. Raccoons use abandoned dens of woodchucks, skunks, and foxes to raise their kits. Raccoons also nest in gaps in trees or caves. Great horned owls recycle nests from squirrels, crows, hawks, and other large birds.

fox kits

Shape Fakers

Some spiders and insects hide from hungry birds by pretending to be part of flowers, leaves, or twigs. These types of animals are called mimics.

Colorful Surprise

Ring-neck snakes live in leaf litter and under fallen logs and rocks, feeding on insects and earthworms. They rarely grow longer than 12 inches or wider than your pinky finger. Ring-necks do not have venom to protect themselves, so they stay out of sight, camouflaging in soil and leaves. If a predator threatens a ring-neck, they roll over and curl up their tails, showing brightly colored undersides that mimic the colors of animals with toxins.

Flower Power

Hungry birds and spiders are always on the lookout for small frogs. Flowers make safe places to hide, sleep, and have a drink. When insects visit the blooms for nectar, the frogs also get a meal.

leopard

Spots & Stripes

Spots provide camouflage by breaking up the outlines of an animal's body. The spots are formed when a mutation in their DNA breaks up the stripe patterns. The same groups of DNA base pairs code for stripes and spots in domestic tabby cats.

Defense **WOW!**

Spots in Disguise

Leopard frog spots blend in well with duckweed.

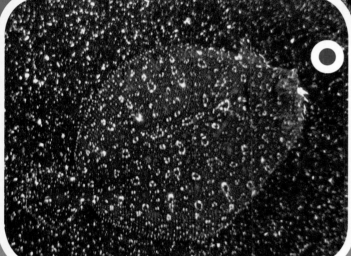

Changing Colors

Flounder fish use special color cells to help them camouflage with patterns on ocean floors. Cuttlefish, octopuses, and chameleons also use these cells.

Hide 'n Seek

There are more than 10,000 species of grass-hoppers, and most of them blend in well with their environments. Which grasshoppers leave more offspring, the ones that blend in well, or the ones that do not?

Bite-Proof Armor

Armadillos wear layers of protein-covered bones called scutes (skootz) like armor for protection from the teeth and venom of predators. The armor also works like an exoskeleton, protecting them from rocky surfaces and thorns. Armadillos do not have scutes on their abdomens, so they often sleep in curled-up positions.

In some places, armadillos are an invasive species, and have damaged wildlife by eating turtle and quail eggs. Armadillos also damage the environment by digging many holes when foraging for beetles.

Stand Back!

Skunks defend themselves with a smelly, oily liquid that comes from glands under their tails. Skunks can aim their spray more than ten feet away! Skunks use their spray with care — they would rather just threaten to spray because it takes their bodies several days to make more. Skunks often stay in their dens while their bodies make more spray.

Confusing Tails

Longhorn sheep, like many of their close relatives, have interesting fur colors near their tails. These colorations help them blend in with their environment, and confuse predators when the sheep run in zigzag patterns.

Defense WOW!

Herd Haven

Many animals, including these wild horses, protect themselves by living in groups called herds. Research with zebras, which are close relatives of horses, showed that females live in stable herds when there is a lot of food and water. When food and water are less available, the zebras tend to spread out.

Sound Effects

Dolphins and whales use clicks, whistles, and pulses to communicate with each other. Individuals have unique sounds, and so do pods. These sounds are made with air sacs under their blowholes.

Sounds also help whales and dolphins find food with echolocation. Like bats, they can measure the timing and the type of sound waves that return, which tells them where solid objects such as fish or seals are, and how far away they are.

dolphins

Defense WOW!

Safety in Numbers

Both dolphins and orcas (above) live in family groups called pods. Living in pods has many benefits. Pods provide protection from predators. Pod members help moms care for calves, and pod members also hunt together, helping them catch food they might not be able to get if they hunted alone.

snow monkeys

Bug Off!

Most female primates hold their babies near both day and night for protection and for feeding. Moms also spend a lot of time grooming their babies to remove insects and other parasites.

Defense WOW!

meerkats

orangutans

Costly Care

Protecting your offspring by keeping it safely with you may seem like a good strategy, but it has a cost. How many babies can a primate hold at the same time? Not many! Female orangutans usually only have one baby every eight years, and only four or five in their lifetimes. Compare those numbers to insects or fish that can lay hundreds of thousands of eggs in their lifetimes.

Extended Family

Baby elephants stay close to their moms and to other females in their herd. Healthy, adult elephants do not have predators, but lions and hyenas attack young elephants when they get the chance.

Defense WOW!

Stand Near

Like many other large mammals, female giraffes have very few offspring, but guard them very well. Male calves stay with their moms for about 15 months, while females may live in their mom's herd for the rest of their lives.

Free Ride

Parent swans protect their young cygnets for about six months. Predators include turtles, large fish, foxes, crows, herons, and magpies. Both moms and dads let their young ride on their backs when the cygnets become tired or when predators are nearby.

Seatbelts, Please!

Baby opposums from North America and possums from Australia and New Zealand get some amazing rides from their moms. As marsupials, they spend their early days in their mother's pouch. When they get older, they ride on mom's back!

Learn from Mom

Mongoose moms raise their young in dens. As they get older, the moms take the pups out to learn how to hunt. Mongooses are famous for attacking and eating snakes such as cobras.

Foraging WOW!

FORAGING: the act of searching for food

From sweet flower nectar to fresh-caught fish, animal foraging can make you say WOW! Instincts, learned behavior, and body adaptations help animals find the food they use to make energy.

Great Escapes

Brown bears, including this grizzly, catch prey by striking it with the large, flat surface of their front paws. Grizzlies also catch fish by swimming underwater with the fish and biting them when they swim too close.

Foraging WOW!

Snow Cones

Many animals, including this bison and deer, eat snow every day in the winter to get water without traveling to streams and rivers. Bison often feed on roots and grasses under the snow.

bison

deer

Great Predators

Cheetahs may get the lion's share of the credit for fast feline runs, but leopards are fast movers, too. Leopards can leap more than twenty feet in one jump, and can run more than thirty-five miles per hour for short distances. Like many other carnivores, leopards also use their whiskers to recognize prey from non-prey. Just a light brush of their whiskers over a surface can tell them whether an item is a living animal, a dead animal, or something such as a rock that was never alive.

Foraging WOW!

Room with a View

Herons, egrets, and cormorants stand on hippopotamuses as they search for fish. Adult hippos have no predators, making their backs a safe perch.

Hard Work

Being a plant-eating herbivore may seem much easier than being a meat-eating carnivore. After all, your food cannot run away from you when you're hungry, and aside from a few pesky thorns, plants do not fight back.

Eating plants may seem easy, but digesting them is hard work. The cell walls in plants are made from cellulose, which is very difficult to digest. Also, compared to the proteins and fats in carnivore foods, the sugars in plants provide much less energy, so herbivores must spend more time eating.

koala bear

red panda

Foraging WOW!

No Cud Chewing Here

Plant-eating mammals such as the rabbit, elephant, and orangutans shown here spend most of their awake time searching for food and eating.

Nectar Snacks

Nectar bats use their hollow, tube-like tongues the way we use soda straws, sucking high-sugar nectar from deep inside flowers. A nectar bat's tongue is so long that it cannot fit inside its mouth. Instead, part of the tongue stays in the bat's rib cage when it is not eating.

Skull Space

Long, thin beaks protect a hummingbird's tongue so it can feed on nectar that most other animals cannot reach. Their tongues are so long that they do not fit in their beaks and mouths. Instead, hummingbirds store part of their tongues in a hollow space in their skulls!

Foraging WOW!

Many Mouths to Feed

Great egret nestlings have a thick layer of fluffy down feathers. Their parents return to the nest after eating, and regurgitate their food into the chicks' mouths. When the chicks get older, parents let chicks take fresh-caught food directly from their beaks. The largest nestlings feed first, and often get more food than their smaller siblings.

Group Effort

Pelicans often hunt together, swimming in rows or horseshoe shapes to herd fish into smaller and smaller spaces, making them easier to catch.

Fly-Through Lane

Great egrets hunt while wading, swimming, and flying. They spear fish and insects with their sharp beaks, and also steal food from smaller birds.

Upside Down

How long could you eat your dinner hanging up-side down? Not as long as a parrot! Their feet have extra-strong muscles and tendons that keep them from falling.

Amphibian Snacks

Although many birds eat insects and worms, some species prefer larger prey such as salamanders, newts, and frogs.

Foraging WOW!

Snake Bites

How does a bird catch snakes? Very carefully! Actually, birds are well adapted for snake catching. Their feet are protected from bites by scales and feathers, and their beaks are made of keratin, like your fingernails. Some birds kill snakes by dropping them many times. Other birds, such as this owl, use their beaks to cut off the snake's air supply so they cannot breathe. Birds with strong feet sometimes stand on snakes to suffocate them.

Double Duty

When birds eat berries, the fruit's sugars give them energy. Most birds cannot digest the seeds inside the fruit, so the seeds leave their bodies as waste in their feces. Berry-eating birds help plants by dispersing and fertilizing their seeds.

Handle with Care

Osprey parents feed their young small pieces of fresh-caught fish. Like other raptors, the flesh-tearing hooks on their beaks are covered in nerve cells that help parents gently place food in their nestlings' mouths.

Foraging WOW!

Sibling Rivalry

Blue jay parents (right) feed whole insects to their nestlings. Which bird do you think will get this grasshopper?

woodpeckers

Food Fights!

Pileated woodpecker parents bring food to their chicks all day long. The parents bring whole ants and beetle larvae to older chicks, called fledglings. For younger chicks, called hatchlings and nestlings, the parents regurgitate partially digested insects and place them in their chicks' mouths.

Eating Machines

Caterpillars spend most of their time feeding and searching for food. Why are they so hungry? They need to store extra energy to go through metamorphosis, when their larval forms change into winged adults.

Stronger Than Steel

Not all spiders spin webs, but those that do use them to catch prey. Different species (types) of web-spinning spiders spin different types of webs, depending on where they live and what type of prey they are trying to catch.

Foraging WOW!

Stinging Snack

Marine turtles can feed on jellyfish and close relatives of jellyfish, such as anemones, without being stung.

Wild Venom

Coleman shrimp live in Indo-Pacific oceans. Their exoskeletons camouflage well with fire urchins. Although these sea urchins have venomous spines, Coleman shrimp can eat them without getting sick.

Lapping Tongues

Honeybees use their long tongues (called a proboscis) to lap up nectar from flowers. Filled with high-energy sugar, bees bring the nectar back to their hives.

Coiled Tongues

Butterflies and moths use long, hollow tongues to suck nectar from plants. Like nectar bats and hummingbirds, butterfly and moth tongues are too large to fit in their mouths. Instead, they keep them rolled up in a coil outside of their bodies.

Razor Tongues

Snails use the sharp edges of their tongues (called a radula) to scrape food from seeds, flowers, and fruits. Some species are carnivores, and eat earthworms, amphibian eggs, and other snails.

Anatomy WOW!

ANATOMY: the shapes and structures of organisms

From whiskers to flippers, animal anatomy can make you say WOW! Anatomy adaptations help animals make homes, get food, fight predators, and more.

sea lion

Built-In Flippers

Many aquatic mammals have webbing between their fingers and toes that helps them swim faster. Webbed hands and feet work like snorkel fins and boat oars, giving the animals extra surface to push through the water.

Spread out your fingers and toes and imagine them with webbed skin between them. How many animals can you think of that have webbed feet or hands? Do they all live near water?

sea otter

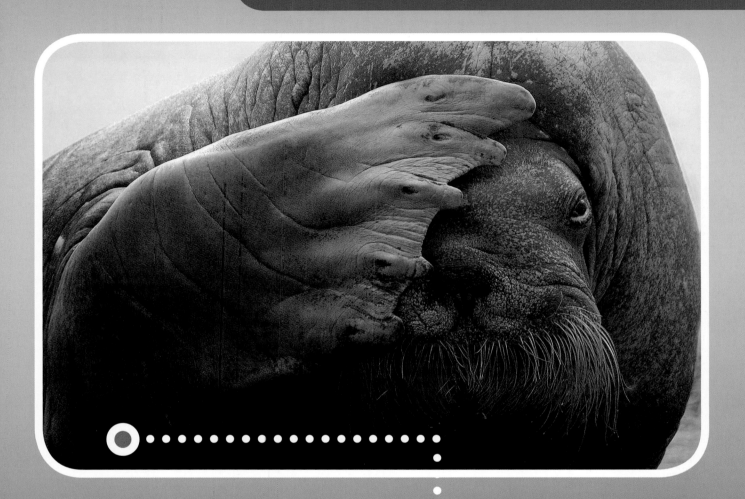

Whisker Beards

Walrus whiskers grow downward, not sideways, and there are lots of them. Although they may look a little silly, these whisker beards help walruses sense nearby water movements by predators and prey.

Big Brains

Despite their name, cuttlefish are close relative of squid and octopuses, not fish. They have large brains and are good problem solvers. Cuttlefish use their eight arms and two tentacles like hands to grasp and twist shells and other items.

Strong Suckers

Like cuttlefish, octopuses are smart carnivores with suckers on their tentacles. When the suckers press against prey, the muscles contract. The suckers have millions of neurons (nerve cells) in them, which helps them apply and release force at just the right time in just the right place.

Clever Camouflage

Just like some land animals, many underwater animals camouflage themselves to look like parts of their environment. Some look like seaweeds, some look like corals, and others look like anemones. These shapes and colors provide camouflage, helping the animals hide from predators and prey.

Look at the fish on this page and the sea dragon on the facing page. Are these camouflage adaptations perfect? Suppose all of the coral or seaweed in these animals' environments died? Would these camouflages still work?

frogfish

rockfish

rockfish

Surprise Disguise

Leafy sea dragons are a type of fish that live in Australia. Their leaf-like body shapes help them blend in with seaweed.

Coral Hideouts

Blennies have long, slim bodies that help them fit in holes and crevices in dead corals. The colors and patterns of their scales often blend in well with the corals they live in.

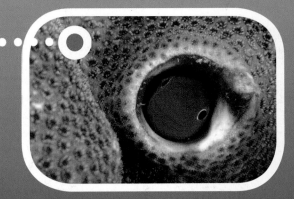

No Warts Here

Alligators and crocodiles use special sense organs all over their bodies called dermal pressure receptors to locate prey in water and on land. These receptors can also pick up low-frequency sounds from other alligators and crocodiles. Dermal receptors may look like bumps or warts, but they are really high-tech communication tools!

Anatomy WOW!

Warning Tails

Rattlesnakes use rings of keratin at the tips of their tails as a warning defense when they feel threatened. Keratin is the protein in your finger-nails — can you rattle your finger-nails when you feel afraid?

Better to Lose a Tail Than a Life . . .

Like some other lizards, anoles can surrender their tail to a predator and regrow a new one.

Worm Snakes

These small, worm-like snakes live in moist places, often under rocks and leaves. They use smooth scales and the tip of their tails to help them burrow through soil.

gull

Defying Gravity

Birds often look like they are headed for a crash landing right before they catch prey. Instead of crashing into the ground head-first, they change directions at the very last second. How do they do this? With unusual skeletons, that's how! Many of their bones are fused together, giving a stronger surface for big muscles to attach onto.

Anatomy WOW!

eagle

Extra-Strong Feet!

The claws on birds of prey are called talons. Strong muscles and tendons lock the talons in place when birds fly away with prey. Biologists estimate that the grip strength of a bird's talons is about ten times stronger than the grip strength of a human hand.

Sleep Tight . . .

Many birds hang onto tree branches by wrapping three toes around the front of the branch and one toe around the backside. A tendon in their ankle locks their feet in place so they do not fall, even when sleeping.

Multi-Tasking Noses

An elephant's trunk is formed by adaptations to its upper lip and its nose. The trunk can be used like an extra arm for grasping, pulling, and lifting. Elephants also use their trunks for communication with other elephants, for guiding their young, and for spraying mud, water, and dust on themselves. An elephant's trunk has more than 15,000 muscles!

Anatomy WOW!

Pouch Protection

Young wallabies and kangaroos, called joeys, use pouches inside their moms as a safe refuge from predators. Newborn joeys crawl up their mother's abdomens to the pouch, and then they attach to a nipple to nurse. Newborn joeys spend all of their time in the pouch. Older joeys spend more time outside as they become more independent.

Hump Days

Adult camels eat grasses and shrubs. Young camels drink high-sugar milk from their moms. Their humps store extra fat, not water.

Gene Switches

Many animals have genes that are turned on and off because of something in their environment. Arctic foxes, for example, change their coat colors during the year.

In the winter, genes for making colored coats are turned off, and the foxes blend in well with the snow around them, helping them find food and avoid predators.

When temperatures get warmer and there's more sunlight from longer days, genes for colored fur are turned on, making fur coats that blend in well with spring and summer environments.

Anatomy WOW!

moose

gazelle

Handy Headwear

Animals use horns and antlers to tell other animals how strong and healthy they are. They also use them to fight.

bighorn sheep

Cool Differences

Not all horns and antlers are the same. Gazelle horns grow in tight rings. Bighorn sheep horns grow backward, and can weigh more than thirty pounds. Moose antlers can grow more than six feet wide!

Bear Scents

Like many other mammals, bears use the moist area inside their noses to pick up scent molecules. Bears have more than one hundred times more smelling space in their noses than humans do. Bears can also pick up scents with the Jacobson's organ in the roof of their mouths. Do you know of any reptiles that use Jacobson's organs to smell?

Bears use their amazing sense of smell to recognize other bears and to find prey. One study showed bears can smell prey from forty miles away.

Long Noses

Elephant shrews have an extra-long, elephant-like snout that helps them find insects. They live in Africa, and can run upright, on their back feet!

Snow-Tunnel Scents

Pine martens use their strong sense of smell to hunt for mice, voles, and chipmunks through tunnels under snow. In the summer, martens add nuts and berries to their diet.

Thousands Of Noses?

Moths have feather-like antennae with thousands of smell receptors on them. Some moths can smell chemicals more than seven miles away!

Exoskeleton Colors

Exoskeletons do more than provide protection for arthropods such as this crab and spider. They also let the animals compete better by helping them blend in with their environments or send warnings to predators.

Anatomy WOW!

Helmet Heads

Treehoppers are known for the helmet-like shape of their bodies. There are more than 3,000 species (types) of treehoppers. Some species have helmets that look like seeds, thorns, and even ants.

Sweet Tricks

The orchid mantis was named because it looks like an orchid flower. Its flower-like colors and shapes trick pollinating insects into thinking they will get a meal. Instead, the orchid mantis makes the insects its meal.

Round Ears?

The large circle near this frog's eye is called a tympanic (tim-pan-ick) membrane. Frogs use this organ to hear other frogs calling, and to sense air movements from predators and prey.

Hair Adaptations

Porcupines use their stiff hairs — called quills — for defense. An average North American porcupine has about 30,000 quills, and every quill has hundreds of barbs at its tip, making them difficult to remove. If you have a cat or a small dog as a pet, stare at them for a few minutes and try to imagine how 30,000 quills could fit on their body.

Toe Tales

A frog's toes and feet are well adapted to where it lives. Tree frogs have suction-cup discs on their toes that help them climb and grip many surfaces. Frogs and toads that dig dens have sharp, claw-like toes, while frogs that live near water have webbing between their toes.

SCAVENGER HUNT CHALLENGES

Snakes from all over the world are often found in coiled-up positions. **SCAVENGER HUNT CHALLENGES:** Inside, search through your imagination for possible reasons why snakes might spend so much time in coils. How many ideas did you come up with? Next, ask your school librarian to help you do some research to find out what snake scientists say.

Many animals need caves and dens for protection. Here, a porcupinefish and a moray eel are sharing a cave. **SCAVENGER HUNT CHALLENGES:** Inside, do an image search for "animals and caves and dens" and find at least five kinds of animals that use caves and dens. Outside, find a cave or a den, but do not put any part of your body in it!

SCAVENGER HUNT CHALLENGES

Many plant-eating insects, including this grasshopper, are camouflaged from predators by the plants they eat. **SCAVENGER HUNT CHALLENGES:** Inside, do an information search for "insects and herbivory." Outside, find at least five leaves that show signs (bite marks!) of an insect herbivore eating them.

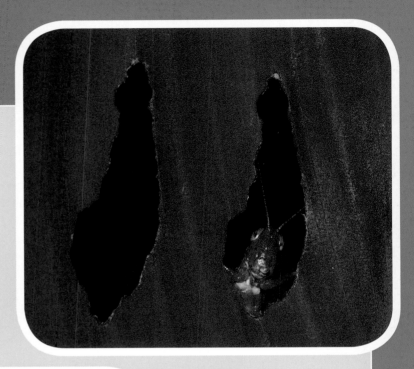

Snow monkeys spend parts of their days soaking in hot springs in Jigokudani Monkey Park in Japan. **SCAVENGER HUNT CHALLENGES:** Inside, do an information search for "Jigokudani Monkey Park" to find out more about the monkeys and the park. Outside, find at least three types of animals cleaning themselves. You may have the most success if you sit quietly to watch an animal for a while, instead of just walking around searching for grooming animals.

READ MORE

AMAZING ANIMAL COMMUNICATORS by John Townsend; Raintree (2012).

ANIMAL SNACKS by Dawn Cusick; EarlyLight Books (2012).

ANIMALS THAT MAKE ME SAY OUCH! by Dawn Cusick; Imagine/Charlesbridge (2014).

LEAPS AND CREAPS by Robin Koontz; Marshall Cavendish Benchmark; (2011).

WHAT IN THE WILD by David Schwartz and Yael Schy; Random House Children's Books (2011).

FROM THE NATIONAL WILDLIFE FEDERATION:

Fun on the web:
http://www.nwf.org/Kids/Games.aspx for a world of kids' fun

Magazines: **RANGER RICK** and **RANGER RICK JR.**

Adaptation: A change in an organism's behavior or form that helps it compete better.

Behavior: The ways organisms act.

Carnivore: An animal that eats other animals.

Communication: The sharing of information. Some organisms communicate with sounds or movements, while others communicate with colors or chemicals.

Diffusion: The movement of gasses or liquids from places of higher concentration to places of lower concentration.

Ecosystem: The living and nonliving parts of an environment functioning together.

Habitat: The home for an organism or a group of organisms.

Hatchling: An animal that has recently hatched from eggs.

Herbivore: An animal that eat plants.

Keratin: A type of protein that makes up beaks, feathers, scales, claws, fur, hair, and more.

Larva/Larvae (singular/plural): The worm-like, wingless stage of some types of newly hatched insects.

Parasite: An organism that uses other organisms for food and habitat.

Plankton: The group of living and nonliving things that float on the surface of large bodies of water. Plankton is the foundation of the world's food chain, and contains a lot of eggs, seeds, and algae.

Predator: An organism that preys on other organisms.

Prey: An animal being hunted or eaten by another animal.

Regurgitate: To vomit partially digested food.

Solitary: Living or acting alone.

Territory: An area that an organism lives in and defends.

Toxin: A poisonous substance produced by organisms to help defend themselves from predators or to help them kill prey.

Venom: Poison used by an organism as part of its defense or to find food that is moved through a bite or a sting.

RESEARCH

The author would like to thank and acknowledge the following scientists, organizations, and institutions for their research assistance.

African Elephant Specialist Group, Alaska Department of Fish and Game, American Association for the Advancement of Science, American Bear Association, American Museum of Natural History, Paul L. R. Andrews, Anole Annals, Archa Aouane, G. Thomas Bancroft, Denise Boggs, Gary Brown, Burke Museum (University of Washington), California Academy of Sciences Department of Ornithology and Mammology, Jessica D. Cande, Allison June Barlow Chaney, Clemson Cooperative Extension, Connecticut Department of Environmental Protection, Cornell Lab of Ornithology, Katherine Harmon Courage, Lucas DeGroote, Helose D. Dufour, Duke Marine Lab, Echinoblog, Encyclopedia of Life, Explorit Science Center, Fernbank Science Center, Michaela Florini, Crystal Gammon, Brian Giddings, Ian Gill, Giraffe Conservation Foundation, Nicolas Gompel, Theresa Hague, William Hamilton, Steve Harris, Dan Hartman, Hawk Quest, James Helfield, Melanie Hocine, Jeff Humphries, Illinois Department of Natural Resources, iNaturalist, Internet Center for Wildlife Damage Management (Cornell University, Clemson University, University of Nebraska-Lincoln, and Utah State University), Jeffrey Karp, Victoria A. Kassner, W. M. Kier, Lindsey Konkel, Konstanze Krueger, D. Li, LiveScience, Christopher Mah, MarineBio Conservation Society, Marshall University Department of Herpetology, Donald A. McCrimmon, John R. Meyer, Caroline Minervino, Minnesota Department of Natural Resources, Russell Mizell, National Wildlife Federation, NOAA Fisheries, Y. Norma-Rashid, North American Bear Center, North Carolina Public Broadcasting, North Carolina State University, North Carolina Wildlife Resources Commission, Holly Ober, John C. Ogden, J. C. O'hanlon, Princeton University, Benjamin Prud'homme, Galen B. Rathbun, Jason Read, San Diego Zoo, Elizabeth Schleichert, Science Now, Matthew Shepherd, A. M. Smith, The Swan Sanctuary, University of Florida Department of Entomology, University of Illinois Extension, University of Michigan Animal Diversity Web, USGS Patuxent Wildlife Research Center, WhoZoo, William Wood, Xerces Society, and Yellowstone National Park.

PHOTO CREDITS

The author would like to thank the following photographers for their creative contributions.

From the National Wildlife Federation Photography Archives:

Majed S. Ali, Susannah Alle, Mohammad Al-Saleh, Grant Atkinson, Jeffrey Bange, Swarup Kumar Bera, Kerrie L. Best, Val Blakely, Nancy Blaydes, Ken Blye, John Bomar Jr., Maggie Bond, Gerry Buckel, Tracey Butcher, Howard Cheek, Nina Chung, Kendra J. Crowell, Christopher Crowley, Reg Daves, Pamela Day, Sue Donnelly, Michael Drake, William Drake, Stanley Duncan, Jack Dysart, Nil Eren, Pamela Finnegan, Bonnie Flamer, Barbara Fleming, Eileen Fonferko, Nancy Forester, Mary A. Fusco, Kate Henderson, Eleanor Hilton, Syed Noor Hossain, Dayne Johnson, Diana C. Johnson, Katie Jones, Gloria Keeslar, Mark Kielich, Brett Klaproth, Istvan Keller Korneuburgerstr, David Krzyzak, Panagiotis Laskarakis, Dennis Von Linden, Sara Lopez, Jonathan Lavan/www. underpressurephotog.com, Chuanxiao Li, Theodore Mattas, Megan McCoy, Tripp McCoy, Rick Miller, Jack Nevitt, Walter Nussbaumer, Ocean Allies, Rob Palmer, Joanne Panizzera, Peggy S. Patterson, Natalya Pluzhnikov, Jeff Randall, George W. Ritchey, Carolyn Ross, Joan Saba, Jennifer Sagerman, Eric Sause, Jerry Segraves, Christine Shields, Angela Smith, David Stealey, Jan Steiner, Diann Stewart, Nicholas Thompson, Patrick Tobin, Cesar Tuason, William Tucek, Greg Tucker, Dennis Vandermeersch, Alex Varani, Timothy P. Vidrine, Paul F. Wagner, Jeffery P. Waldorff, Annemarie Walsh, Christopher Welsh, David C. Wilson, Dawn Wilson, Pamela G. Winegar, Richard Winegar, J. L. Wooden, and Minghui Yuan

From Shutterstock:

Alle, Andre Anita, Michal Bednarek, BMJ, Vittorio Bruno, Steve Byland, Rich Carey, Michiel de Wit, Sergey Dubrov, Ericlefrancais, FAUP, GeorgeM Photography, Donna Heatfield, Sandy Hedgepeth, HNC Photo, Irinak, Eric Isselee, Matt Jeppson, Anan Kaewkhammul, Mirek Kijewski, Kazakov Maksim, Erik Mandre, Gerald Marella, Antoni Murcia, Outdoorsman, Arnon Polin, Paul St. Clair, Tracy Starr, Aleksey Stemmer, Tratong, Mike Truchon, and Ye Choh Wah